Mackay v. Dillon

JOHN CATRON

Published in 1846@MACKAY V. DILLON

TABLE OF CONTENTS

PUBLISHED IN 1846MACKAY V. DILLON

JACQUE MACKAY.
'St. Louis, October 9, 1799.'
'St. Louis of Illinois, October 9, 1799.
'Cognizance being taken of the foregoing memorial of Mr. James Mackay, and due attention being paid to his merits and good services, the surveyor of this Upper Louisiana, Don Antonio Soulard, shall put the interested party into possession of the land which he solicits, in the place designated in this memorial, and this being executed, he shall draw a plat of his survey, delivering the same to the party, with his certificate, in order that it shall serve to him to obtain the concession and title in form, from the intendant-general, to whom alone corresponds, by royal order, the distributing and granting all classes of lands of the royal domain.
CARLOS DEHAULT DELASSUS.
'Truly translated. St. Louis, 20th February, 1833.
JULIUS DE MUN.'
Translation of the Spanish Survey.
'The bounds and corners are all indicated on the survey. All the line-trees are marked with a blaze above, and two notches below, and the right and left blazed only. Marked in book A, fol. 55, No. 94.
'Don Antoine Soulard, particular surveyor of Upper Louisiana, certify that, on the 24th of this present year, in virtue of the decree which accompanies of the Lieutenant-Governor and subdelegate of the royal estate, Don Carlos Dehault Delassus, in date of the month of October, of the year 1799, I went to the land of Don Santiago Mackay, the admeasurement of which I have taken in presence of the proprietor and of the neighbours who bound

thereon, with the perch of Paris of eighteen feet long, according to the custom adopted in this province of Louisiana, and without regarding the variations of the needle, which is seven (7) degrees and thirty (30) minutes, as appears by the plat that precedes; which land is situate to the south of the little river of the mills, situate near the town of St. Louis, bounding north by the lands of Don Auguste Chouteau; south, in part, by another piece of land of Don Antonio Soulard and the royal domain; east, in part, by the land of Don Auguste Chouteau, and by the royal road from the town to the village of Carondelet; west, by the lands of the royal domain; and in order that it may appear when fitting, I give the present with the plat that precedes, in which are indicated the dimensions and natural and artificial limits which surround the said land. St. Louis of Illinois, 17th of December, 1802.

ANTONIO SOULARD Particular Surveyor.'4. Proceedings of the board of commissioners established by the act of Congress, passed the 2d of March, 1805.

This act provided for the appointment of three persons, who should examine and decide on all claims submitted to them, and report the result to the Secretary of the Treasury, who was directed to communicate it to Congress.

'July 22d, 1806.

'The board met agreeably to adjournment. Present the Honorable John B. C. Lucas, Clement B. Penrose, and James L. Donaldson, Esquires.

'James Mackay, claiming two hundred arpents of land, or thereabouts, situate in the fields of St. Louis, produces a concession from Charles D. Delassus, dated October 9th, 1799, and a survey of the same, dated the 24th of November, and certified the 17th of December, 1802.

'Auguste Chouteau, being duly sworn, says, that the said tract of land was surveyed in 1804 or 1805; that he never heard of a concession having been granted for the same until the survey was taken; that the said tract is adjoining a tract claimed by the witness, and that the same interferes with a tract claimed by the inhabitants of St. Louis as a common. The board, from the above testimony, are satisfied that the aforesaid concession is antedated. On motion, adjourned to to-morrow, 9 o'clock, A. M. See minutes, No. 1, pp. 412, 413, 417, and 419.'

'Friday, July 31st, 1807. 3 o'clock.

'The board met agreeably to adjournment. Present the Honorable John B. C. Lucas, Clement B. Penrose, and Frederick Bates, Esquires. James Mackay, claiming about two hundred and eighty-two arpents in the common of St. Louis, produces a concession from Charles Dehault Delassus, dated the 9th of October, 1799. Survey and certificate dated the 17th of December, 1802. Laid over for decision. The board adjourned until to-morrow, 9 o'clock.

JOHN B. C. LUCAS.
CLEMENT B. PENROSE.
FREDERICK BATES.
'See book No. 3, pp. 19-21.'
'Saturday, November 4th, 1809.
'Board met. Present, John B. C. Lucas, Clement B. Penrose, commissioners. James Mackay, claiming two hundred and eighty-two arpents of land, situate on the commons of St. Louis. See book No. 1, p. 417; book No. 3, p. 21. It is the opinion of the board that this claim ought not to be confirmed. Board adjourned till Monday next, 9 o'clock, A. M.
JOHN B. C. LUCAS.
CLEMENT B. PENROSE.
'See book No. 4, pp. 185-187.'5. Proceedings under the act of the 13th of June, 1812.
'St. Louis, December 28th, 1813.
'James Mackay claims about thirty arpents of land near the town of St. Louis, produces a concession from Charles D. Delassus, Lieutenant-Governor, for about two hundred arpents, dated the 9th of October, 1799. Survey of two hundred and eithty-eight arpents, 17th of December, 1802 (certified).
'M. P. Leduc, as agent of claimant, abandons all but about thirty arpents; the part abandoned supposed to be comprehended by the survey of the commons. It appearing from the minutes, book No. 1, p. 417, that no testimony has been introduced on the merits of this claim. A witness is now admitted.
'Antoine Soulard, duly sworn, says that this claim was granted to claimant by C. D. Delassus, Lieutenant-Governor, on the recommendation of his successor, Z. Suedeau, who had promised the same. It was surveyed under the Spanish government, and has ever since been considered as property of claimant; that corn was raised on premises for claimant, during three or four of the last years.
'Note. No more abandoned than may fall within the commons, should they be confirmed. See Bates's minutes, pp. 116 117.'
6. Extracts from the decision of Mr. Bates under the same act, and act of 3d March, 1813.
Plaintiffs then read in evidence extracts from Bates's decision, opinions of the recorder of land titles for Missouri Territory, as to claims entered under act of 13th June, 1812, and proven before 1st January, 1814, as provided by the act of the 3d of March, 1813, comprehending also the claims in the late district of Arkansas, which, by act of 2d August, 1813, were permitted to be entered until 1st January, 1814, and proven until 1st July, 1814, together with the extensions of quantity provided by fourth section of act of 3d March, 1813, and confirmations under the act of 12th April, 1814.

Warrant or Survey Notice to the Quantity Where Poss'n, inhab Opinions
order of sur- recorder by claimed. situated or cultivation. of the re-
vey. whom. corder.
Con. fr. C. 17th Dec., James Mackay. 30 arp's of By cultivation Cultivation
in Confirmed 30 arp's
Delassus, Lt. 1802, for the surplus as falling corn from 1810 O.S.B. p. 417,
N.M.
Gov. 9th Oct. 288 arpents. abandoned com- within the- to 1813. 117. No
More
1779, for mons of Saint abandoned than may
about 200 arp's. Louis. fall within the
commons should they
be confirmed.
'RECORDER'S OFFICE,
St. Louis, Missouri, 5th December, 1840.
'I certify the above to be truly extracted from page 36 of book No. 2, except
the caption, which is truly copied from page 1 of book No. 1, being two of
the five small books, with the following indorsement on the first, and also
on the fifth book, believed to be in the handwriting of Frederick Bates, to
wit:
'These five small books are originals in the proper handwriting of the
undersigned, being his decisions on land claims since the adjournment of
the late board. These were arranged and fairly transcribed for report to the
commissioner of the general land-office, but not yet recorded in the books,
because they have no authority till sanctioned by government.
FREDERICK BATES, Recorder of Land Titles.
'St. Louis, November 1st, 1815.
'All on file in this office.
F. R. CONWAY,
U.S. Recorder of Land Titles in the State of Missouri.'
This decision the plaintiffs alleged to have been confirmed by the act of
29th April, 1816. 3 Lit. and Brown's ed. 328.
7. Proceedings of the board of commissioners, established by the acts of
9th July, 1833, and 2d March, 1833.
The act of 1832 authorized commissioners to examine all the unconfirmed
claims to land in Missouri, andc., to class them, and, at the commencement
of each session of Congress during said term of examination, lay before the
commissioner of the general landoffice a report of the claims so classed,
andc., to be laid before Congress for their final decision upon the claims
contained in the first class. The act of 1833 directed the commissioners to
embrace every claim to a donation of land, held in virtue of settlement and
cultivation.
Plaintiffs then read in evidence, from the report of the recorder and

commissioners for the adjustment of land titles in Missouri, under the acts of Congress of the 9th of July, 1832, and 2d of March, 1833, printed by authority of Congress, all under the head of No. 54 (James Mackay claiming two hundred and more arpents,) pp. 174-177 of said report.

'Monday, February 18th, 1833.

'F. R. Conway, Esq., appeared pursuant to adjournment, having been authorized, by a resolution of the board of commissioners of the 1st of December last, to receive evidence. James Mackay, by his legal representatives, claiming two hundred and more arpents, it being a special location. See book B, pp. 433, 434; minutes, No. 1, p. 417; minutes of recorder, p. 117. The claimant further refers to book B, p. 486, in order to show that the claim for the commons of St. Louis does not interfere with this claim; also, to book No. 5, p. 552. Produces a paper purporting to be a concession from Carlos Dehault Delassus, dated October 9, 1799. See Bates's decision, p. 36.

'M. P. Leduc, being duly sworn, saith, that the signature to concession is in the proper handwriting of the said Carlos Dehault Delassus. Book No. 3, p. 21; No. 4, p. 186. For further testimony of M. P. Leduc in behalf of this claim, see next claim below. Antoine Soulard, claiming two hundred and four arpents forty-eight perches, to wit: deponent further says that he informed Mr. Soulard that in case he would abandon the part of his claim which was included in the commons of St. Louis, Mr. Bates would confirm the balance of said claim; thereupon Soulard called upon Mr. Bates, and made the abandonment, upon which Bates confirmed the part of said claim which lies east of the common, and at the same time, Soulard, as agent for Mackay, made the same abandonment on Mackay's claim, and that since that time Soulard told the deponent that Mackay disapproved of said abandonment, and that he, the said deponent, never acted as agent for Mackay in said claim; that he does not know that Soulard ever was authorized by Mackay to make said abandonment; that since the time of said abandonment, Mackay remained as ostensible owner and claimant of said land; that he built thereon a house, and lived and died in it. The deponent further says, that what he understands by these claims interfering with the commons of St. Louis, is the part of said claims included in the survey of said commons, made by Mackay in 1806, as recorded. Deponent believes that taxes were paid by Mackay and Soulard on said lands until 1820; and that the part of Mackay's claim which was not confirmed was sold under an execution as being the property of said Mackay. Adjourned until to-morrow, at 10 o'clock, A. M.

F. R. CONWAY.'

See book No. 6, pp. 102-104, and 107.

'Thursday, November 7th, 1833.

'The board met pursuant to adjournment. Present, L. F. Linn, A. G.

Harrison, F. R. Conway, commissioners. James Mackay claiming two hundred and more arpents. See p. 103 of this book. The board, after minutely examining the original papers in this case, see no cause for entertaining even the suspicion of the concession being antedated, as expressed by the former board, and they are unanimously of opinion that this claim ought to be confirmed to the said James Mackay, or to his legal representatives, according to the concession. The board adjourned until to-morrow, 9 o'clock, A. M.

L. F. LINN,

F. R. CONWAY.

A. G. HARRISON.'

See book No. 6, pp. 304, 306, and 307.

8. The act of Congress passed 4th July, 1836.

By this act, Congress confirmed the decisions in favor of land claimants made by the above commissioners, saving and reserving, however, to all adverse claimants the right to assert the validity of their claims in a court or courts of justice; and the second section declared, that if it should be found that any tract or tracts thus confirmed, or any part thereof, had been previously located by any other person or persons under any law of the United States, or had been surveyed or sold by the United States, the present act should confer no title to such lands in opposition to the rights acquired by such location or purchase, andc., andc.

9. The certificate of the surveyor of the public lands, dated 5th December, 1840, accompanying which was a plat.

'St. Louis, 5th of December, 1840.

'The above plat of survey No. 3, 123, containing 225 10/100 acres, in the name of James Mackay, or his legal representatives, is correctly copied from the approved plat on file in this office. The said survey is the tract confirmed to said James Mackay, or his legal representatives, by the act of Congress, approved the 4th of July, 1836, entitled 'An act confirming claims to land in the State of Missouri, and for other purposes,' it being No. 54 in the report of the commissioners referred to in the above designated act of Congress. No separate survey has been made of the thirty arpents of said tract, confirmed by an act of Congress, approved the 29th of April, 1816.

WILLIAM MILBURN,

Surveyor of the Public Lands of the States of Illinois and Missouri.'

10. The deposition of Soulard.

Plaintiffs then read in evidence the deposition of Garlon Soulard, namely:

'We do hereby agree, that the deposition of James G. Soulard be taken on this 30th of November, 1839, to be read in evidence in the trial of a certain cause now pending in the Circuit Court of St. Charles county, State of Missouri, wherein the heirs of James Mackay, deceased, are plaintiffs, and Patrick M. Dillon is defendant. On the part of the plaintiffs, L. E. Lawless;

H. R. Gamble for defendant. James G. Soulard, of lawful age, being produced, sworn, and examined on the part of the plaintiffs, on his oath says, I was very well acquainted with the late James Mackay, who died at his residence in St. Louis county, in the fall or winter of 1823 or 1824; I think in 1823. He left several children, who are still living; namely, Zeno, Eliza, wife of Reuben Coleman, Catherine, wife of Louis Guyon, Julia, wife of David Bowles, Antoine, James, Amelia Ann, wife of William Coleman, Louisa, lately married to some person in Kentucky; whose name is Baker, as I am informed; he also left a widow, who is still living; her name is Isabella L. Mackay. The residence of James Mackay, and where he died, is part of the building now known as the convent, in the south part of the city of St. Louis. The confirmed part of the tract of land on which said house is built is outside and east of the line of the St. Louis commons; and all the land there inclosed and occupied by Mr. Mackay, at the time of his death, was east of the commons. He had about three acres inclosed (as near as I can remember). The part occupied by him was understood to be that part of said land which was confirmed to Mr. Mackay. Mr. Mackay left a will and appointed executors; namely, Anthony Soulard, my father, Isabella L. Mackay, the widow, and Zeno Mackay, under certain conditions, and Gabriel Long. The widow of James Mackay remained in possession of the mansion-house, after the death of her husband, two or three years, I think, by herself and her tenants; after she ceased to occupy it, I think Mr. Mullanply took possession; after which time neither my father nor Mr. Mackay ever had possession of any part of the said tract as executors of James Mackay.

JAMES G. SOULARD.

'Sworn to and subscribed, before me, this 30th of November, A. D. 1839.

P. W. WALSH, Justice.'

11. Proof of the location and value of the land.

Plaintiffs then proved that land in the possession of Dillon was on the east end of the United States survey offered in evidence, west of the dotted line representing front line of commons; that the land on the extreme west end of said survey was worth three hundred dollars per acre, and increased in value as you proceed east in said survey, and that the monthly value of the premises in possession of Dillon was one cent per month. (Here the plaintiffs closed their case.)

The defendant, to sustain his title, gave in evidence the following documents, and referred to the following laws.

1. Proceedings of Syndics.

2. Survey of the tract claimed as commons, by Mackay, in 1806.

3. Proceedings of the board of commissioners under the act of Congress passed in 1805, the same law which was referred to by the plaintiffs, as above mentioned.

4. Act of Congress passed 13th of June, 1812.

5. Act of Congress passed 26th of May, 1824, and the testimony taken under it.

6. Act of Congress passed January 27, 1831.

7. Evidence of Pascal Cerre.

8. Two deeds from the city of St. Louis to Dent and Dillon respectively.

1. Proceedings of Syndics.

'We, the undersigned, Syndics named by the meeting of inhabitants holden in the government-chamber, the 22d of the month of September of this year, 1782, by Mr. Don Francis Cruzat, Lieutenant-Colonel Grad, of infantry, commander-in-chief and lieutenant-governor of the western part and districts of the Illinois, to establish fixed and unalterable rules for the construction and maintenance of the streets, bridges, and canals of this village, clothed with the authority of the public, which have selected us for these ends, have determined in the said government-chamber, and in the presence of the aforesaid Mr. D. F. Cruzat, this day, the 29th of the same month, the following, which is to be regularly conformed to, in future.

'1. There shall be held, the first day of every year, in the government-chamber, and in the presence of Monsieur the Lieutenant-Governor, a meeting of all the inhabitants of this post, wherein, by a plurality of voices, there shall be named two Syndics, who shall together ('unanimously') superintend the maintenance of the streets, bridges, and canals of the village, and who shall be obliged to cause to be observed and fulfilled strictly the following articles.

'2. The first duty of the Syndics, immediately after their election, shall be, to examine for themselves the interior locality of the village, and to cause without delay the streets, canals, and bridges to be repaired by the persons who are bound so to do, and whom we indicate below; and that if any one refuse to conform thereto, they have recourse to law to compel them to fulfil an object so indispensable for the public convenience.

'3. All the inhabitants fronting upon a street along which a run (streamlet) shall pass shall be obliged to give a course to the water to the Mississippi, to make the canals and bridges necessary to maintain them, and keep the streets at all times practicable for the convenience of carriages and public cars.

'4. Besides the specifications in the aforegoing articles, the streets in general shall be repaired and maintained in good condition by the proprietors of the grounds fronting on them, it being understood that those opposite to each other shall co operate in equal portions, if the case require it.

'5. Finally, the little river bridge, as well as all the roads which are outside of the village, shall be made (and) maintained by the public.

'Done and passed in the government-hall, and in the presence of Monsieur the Lieutenant-Governor, who has signed with us the said day and year ut supra.

PERRAULT.

BRAGEAUX.

RENE KIERCERAUX.

AUGUSTE CHOUTEAU.

CHAUVIN.

Ordinary mark of JOSEPH + TAILLON.

Ordinary mark of JOSEPH + MOINVILLE.

'Signed, FRANCIS CRUZAT.'

'We, the undersigned, Syndics named by the meeting of the inhabitants which was holden in the government-chamber, the 22d of the month of September of this year, 1782, by Monsieur Don Francis Cruzat, Lieutenant-Colonel Grad, of infantry, commandant-in-chief and lieutenant-governor of the western part and districts of the Illinois, to establish fixed and unalterable rules for the construction and maintenance of the inclosures of the commons of this village, clothed with the authority which elected us for these ends, have determined in the said government-chamber and in the presence of the aforesaid Mr. Don Francis Cruzat, this day, the 29th of the same month, the following, whereunto conformity for the future shall be regularly observed.

'1. The first day of every year there shall be named publicly in the government-chamber, in the presence of Monsieur the Lieutenant-Governor, a Syndic, and immediately afterwards eight arbiters, who shall make the first examination of the inclosures of the commons.

'2. The inclosures of the said commons shall be made and completed every year by the 15th of April, at the latest, and shall be accepted by the eight arbiters the first Sunday after this fourth.

'3. The aforesaid arbiters shall not accept the inclosures, unless they be constructed in such manner that the animals cannot escape from the common and do damage to the seedings of the inhabitants.

'4. It shall be the duty of the said arbiters to render an account of the examination of the inclosures which they shall have made to the Syndic, who thereupon shall immediately nominate eight others, to verify the exactness or negligence of the first. And if there shall be found inclosures which are not in the condition required to be accepted, and the first arbiters shall not have made their report thereof to the Syndic, they shall be condemned to pay each a fine of ten pounds.

'5. Whensoever it shall come to the knowledge of the Syndic, that any inclosure is not in the state decreed by the third article of this ordinance, it shall be his duty to give notice thereof to the proprietor, in order that, without delay, he may apply to it the proper remedy; and if the latter shall, through caprice or otherwise, neglect this first duty, the Syndic shall cause it to be repaired at his cost.

'6. If the last who shall have made the visit of examination to the inclosure shall not have given notice to the Syndic of the condition in which he shall have found them, and if, in the interval between his visit and that which is subsequently to be made, it shall be proved that the animals have escaped, and that they have done any damage, he shall be forced to pay for it; and if it happen that the Syndic, having been warned of the bad condition of the inclosures, shall have neglected to give notice thereof to the proprietors, then he shall be responsible for the damage, and be constrained to pay it himself. In like manner, in the case of the proprietors of the inclosures having been notified by the Syndic to go and repair them, and their failure to do so immediately, they shall undergo the same penalty.

'7. If it happen that at any time when the animals shall have escaped, and shall have done damage, that several inclosures are defective, in order to remedy the vexatious consequences which usually result from similar facts, it is ordered, that the damages be paid in equal portions by those whose inclosures are defective. Nevertheless, if it should occur that, in the interval between one visit and another, the inclosures having been found in good condition by the Syndic or other persons appointed for that purpose, the animals shall have escaped through any breach made by unknown malefactors, or from any other unexpected event, the damage following thereupon shall rest upon him upon whom it has fallen.

'8. If the animals which shall be turned loose come to be taken up in the fields, without the owners having co operated in their egress, they shall not be held to pay either the caption or the supposed damage which they may have occasioned.

'9. Whensoever it shall be proven, that the gate-keeper shall have allowed animals of any sort whatsoever to escape, by his negligence or otherwise, he shall be forced to pay the damage which may be done.

'10. So soon as the inclosures shall have been accepted, it shall not be permitted to any person whatsoever to pass over them, upon pain of paying for the first offence ten pounds, and for the second twenty-four, and suffer an imprisonment of twenty-four hours.

'11. Malefactors surprised in making a breach in the inclosures, whether to pass themselves, or to allow the animals to pass, whatsoever be the motive, shall be condemned to pay, besides the damages they may have caused, a fine of fifty pounds, and to undergo an imprisonment of fifteen days.

'12. It is ordered, that all those who may find any one committing the crime specified in the preceding article shall give the promptest advice thereof to Monsieur, the Lieutenant-Governor, and shall themselves conduct the criminal to prison, if it be possible for them to arrest him; but if any one, through a mistaken indulgence, or any private interest, shall not strictly fulfil this duty, and if it shall be proven that he has stated to other persons that he had surprised any one in such case, he shall be reputed an accomplice in the crime, and condemned to pay the same fine and damages, and undergo the same privation, as hereinbefore provided.

'13. The proprietors of each inclosure shall be obliged to place thereupon a stamp, with their name in full, under penalty of fifteen pounds fine.

'14. He who takes a horse in the prairie, to make use of him, without the consent of the master, shall be condemned to pay twenty-five pounds fine, and punished with twenty-four hours' imprisonment; and if any unlucky accident shall befall the horse, he shall pay therefor according to the estimate which shall be made thereof.

'15. If horses or animals tied in the prairies break their rope, and come to be taken up in the fields, he who takes them up shall receive five pounds per head; and the proprietor of the land whereon they are so taken shall demand the damages, which shall be assessed to him by the arbiters.

'16. Whensoever it shall be proven, that any one has taken the rope of an animal fastened in the prairie, he shall pay ten pounds therefor, without prejudice to the five pounds for the taking, and the damages which he shall have occasioned, according to the estimate of the arbiters, which shall be made thereof.

'17. It shall not be permitted to any person whatever to tie horses or other animals upon the lands of others, without their consent; otherwise the owner of the land shall seize the animals, and exact of him to whom they belong five pounds per head, and shall have the right to claim the supposed damages which they may have done.

'18. Whensoever any slaves shall be found to have violated any of the foregoing articles, their masters shall pay the fines, costs of taking up, and damages prescribed; and the aforesaid slaves shall be punished with the lash, according to the exigency of the case.

'19. All the fines shall be deposited in the hands of the Syndic, designated by the Lieutenant-Governor, of the two who shall be annually named, for the police and maintenance of the village, and they shall be convertible to the public works of the community.

'Done and passed in the government hall, in the presence of the aforesaid Lieutenant-Governor, who has signed with us the same day and year ut supra.

'Signed, PERRAULT.

RENE KIERCERAUX.

BRAGEAUX.

Ordinary mark of JH. + TAILLON. Ordinary mark of JH. +
MOINVILLE.

CHAUVIN.

AUGUSTE CHOUTEAU.

'FRANC. CRUZAT.'

2. Survey of the tract claimed as commons, by Mackay, in 1806.

'I do certify, that the above plat represents four thousand two hundred and ninety-three arpents of land, situated joining the town of St. Louis, and surveyed by me at the request of the inhabitants of the said St. Louis, who claim the same as their right in common, and at whose request I have included in the said common seven different pretensions of different individuals, as appears on the above plot, besides those which are unknown to me, and not surveyed. Given under my hand at St. Louis, the 22d day of February, 1806.

JAMES MACKAY.

'Received for record, St. Louis, 27th February, 1806.

ANTOINE SOULARD, Surveyor-General of Territory of Louisiana.'

3. Proceedings of the board of commissioners, under the act of Congress, passed in 1805 (2 Lit. and Brown's ed. 324), and in connection with this the second volume of American State Papers, 'Public Lands,' 549, 377.

Copied from the original documents on file and of record, in book B, pages 486-488.

'May 10th, 1806.

'The board met agreeably to adjournment. Present, Honorable Clement B. Penrose, Esq.

'The inhabitants of the town of St. Louis, claiming four thousand two hundred and ninety-three arpents of land as a common, produce a certificate of survey of the same, dated 22d of February, 1806,-a set of regulations of the inhabitants, having for object the keeping in order or repairing of the inclosure of said commons, and imposing penalties on such as should neglect or refuse to repair the same. Said regulations, signed by the then Lieutenant-Governor, Cruzat, and dated September 22d, 1782. Auguste Chouteau, being duly sworn, says, that the inhabitants never had a concession for said commons. That he has always known it as such, although of a much smaller extent at first; that it was first fenced in the year 1764, at the expense of the inhabitants, who always kept it in repair; and further, that every person, inhabitant of the village, was in the habit of pasturing his cattle in the same, and of cutting wood; and further, that he has known the said commons, as surveyed and fenced, for upwards of fifteen years hence. Gregoire Sarpee being sworn, says that he arrived in the country about nineteen or twenty years ago; that he has always known said commons as such; that the same had then acquired its present size; that when he arrived he found the same fenced in, and that every inhabitant was obliged, under certain penalties, to attend to and make such repairs as the said inclosure or fence required; and further, that Sylvester Labbadie having, in the year 1792, obtained a concession for lands forming part of said commons, and having, in consequence thereof, began his improvement of the same, the inhabitants remonstrated against it to the governor, who prevented him from cultivating the same, until such time as the intendant should have decreed otherwise.

'William H. Lecompte, being also sworn, says, that he has been an inhabitant of the country for upwards [of] forty-four years; has known the commons from his first arrival in it. That said commons has increased in proportion to the population of the village; that he has known it of the size it now is for upwards of ten years; that the old commons in included in the present one, and that the regulations passed respecting the same were always considered as laws, and enforced as such; and further, that other regulations were had respecting the same, and also put in force. The board reject this claim, for want of actual inhabitation and cultivation, and a duly registered warrant of survey (carried to page 311 for remarks of the board). See commissioner's minutes, book No. 1, pages 288-290.'

'July 14th, 1806.

'The board met agreeably to adjournment. Present, the Honorable John B. C. Lucas, Clement B. Penrose, James L. Donaldson, Esquires.

'In the case of the commons of St. Louis, pp. 289, 290, the board remark, that this claim originated under the French government; that grants of commons were usual under the French and Spanish governments, and in conformity with their respective laws, they deem it to be equitable under Spanish law. On motion, adjourned to Monday, the 16th instant, 9 o'clock, A. M. See minutes, book No. 1, pp. 310-312.'

'Thursday, January 2d, 1812.

'Board met. Present, John B. C. Lucas, Clement B. Penrose, Frederick Bates, commissioners. Inhabitants of the town of St. Louis, claiming 4,293 arpents of land as a common. See book No. 1, pp. 289, 311.

'It is the opinion of a majority of the board that this claim ought not to be granted; Clement B. Penrose, commissioner, voting for a confirmation thereof under the usages and customs of the Spanish government. Board adjourned till Monday next, nine o'clock, A. M.

JOHN B. C. LUCAS.

CLEMENT B. PENROSE.

FREDERICK BATES.

'See commissioner's minutes, book No. 5, pp. 551-553.'

4. Act of Congress, passed the 13th of June, 1812 (2 Lit. and Brown's ed. 748).

This act, amongst other things, enacted, 'That the rights, titles, and claims to town or village lots, out lots, common field lots, and commons in, adjoining, and belonging to the several towns or villages of Portage des Sioux, St. Charles, St. Louis, andc., andc., which lots have been inhabited, cultivated, or possessed prior to the 20th day of December, 1803, shall be, and the same are hereby, confirmed to the inhabitants of the respective towns or villages aforesaid, according to their several right or rights in common thereto; provided, that nothing herein contained shall be construed to affect the rights of any persons claiming the same lands, or any part thereof, whose claims have been confirmed by the board of commissioners for adjusting and settling claims to land in the said territory.'

5. Act of Congress, passed on the 26th of May, 1824 (4 Lit. and Brown's ed. 5), and the testimony taken under it.

Testimony relating to town and village lots, out lots, and common field lots in, adjoining, or belonging to the several towns or villages of Portage des Sioux, St. Charles, St. Louis, St. Ferdinand, Villa a Robert, Carondelet, Ste. Genevieve, New Madrid, New Bourbon, Little Prairie, and Mine a Burton, in Missouri, and the village of Arkansas, in the Territory of Arkansas, as directed by an act of Congress, passed May 26th, 1824.

THEODORE HUNT, Recorder of Land Titles.

See Hunt's minute book, No. 1, p. 1.

The mayor, aldermen, and citizens of the city of St. Louis produce Henry Douchonquette and Joseph Charleville, for the purpose of having their depositions recorded as relates to the St. Louis commons.

Henry Douchonquette, being duly sworn, says he is sixty-six years of age, and has lived in St. Louis upwards of forty years, and during this time, until the change of government took place, he always knew there was a common belonging to the inhabitants of the town of St. Louis, and that there was a fence round it, and that he has often assisted to make and keep in repair the said fence. As near as he can describe it, it was bounded as follows: The fence began near to where Mr. Reynard now lives, above the town, and run back of the town; and from thence to the Carondelet field fence, or to the River des Peres; and the ground thus taken in was considered the commons.

HENRY DOUCHONQUETTE.

Sworn to before me, November 22d, 1825.

THEODORE HUNT, Recorder of Land Titles.

Joseph Charleville, being duly sworn, says he has resided thirty-five years in the town of St. Louis, and is fifty-five years old, and has had the deposition of Henry Douchonquette read to him, and of his knowledge he knows it to be true.

JOSEPH CHARLEVILLE.

Sworn to before me, November 22d, 1825.

THEODORE HUNT, Recorder of Land Titles.

Mackay Wherry, being duly sworn, says he has truly translated and read to Henry Douchonquette and Joseph Charleville the above depositions before they signed the same, and they said they were true.

M. WHERRY.

Sworn to before me, November 22d, 1825.

THEODORE HUNT, Recorder of Land Titles.

See Hunt's MS. book, No. 3, p. 79.

John Bap, Lorain, senior, being duly sworn, as relates to the commons of St. Louis, says he is about eighty-four years of age, and it is about fifty years since he first came to reside in St. Louis, it being when Piernas was lieutenant-governor of this country; and he, this deponent, says, when he first came to reside at St. Louis, the land fenced in between the Mississippi River and the common field fence (excepting the town and such small grants as were made within the said limits) was a common for the use of the inhabitants of the town of St. Louis; certain he is, that it was always used as such by the inhabitants, from the time he first came to reside in St. Louis until he removed to Florisant, about twenty-five years ago; and this deponent further says, that when he first came to St. Louis, the commons extended to the River des Peres; but after that, when Carondelet was laid out, there was an agreement made between the inhabitants of St. Louis and the inhabitants of Carondelet, that the common field fence of St. Louis should join the common field fence of Carondelet, and that all east of the St. Louis field fence should belong to the inhabitants of St. Louis, and west, to Carondelet.

JOHN BAPTISTE his + mark. LORAIN, Pere.
Sworn to before me, November 23d, 1825.
THEODORE HUNT, Recorder of Land Titles.

Baptiste Dominee, being duly sworn, says he is seventy-five years of age, and will have resided forty-six years in St. Louis next February, and that he has had the deposition of John Baptiste Lorain, pere, read to him, and that he knews it to be true.

BAPTISTE his + mark. DOMINEE.
Sworn to before me, November 3d, 1825.
THEODORE HUNT, Recorder of Land Titles.

Alexander Gremaux, dit Charpentier, being duly sworn, says he is sixty-six years of age, and has resided in St. Louis forty-four years, and has heard read to him the deposition of Johh B. Lorain, senior, and knows it to be true; and he further knows, that the commons was surveyed by Antoine Soulard, in the time of the Spanish government.

ALEXANDER his + mark. GREMAUX, dit Charpentier.
Sworn to before me, November 23d, 1825.
THEODORE HUNT, Recorder of Land Titles.

Mackay Wherry, being duly sworn, says, that he has truly translated and read to John Baptiste Lorain, senior, the aforegoing deposition of his, before he signed the same, and that he said it was true; and the he likewise translated and read to Baptiste Dominee and Alexander Gremaux, dit Charpentier, the deposition of John Baptiste Lorain, senior, and that they said it was, to their knowledge, true; and this deponent further says, that he has translated and read the depositions of Baptiste Dominee and Alexander Gremaux to each of them before they signed the same.

M. WHERRY.

Sworn to before me, November 23d, 1825.

THEODORE HUNT, Recorder of Land Titles.

See Hunt's minutes, book No. 3, page 82 and 83.

Baptiste Rivier e del Bacan e, being duly sworn, in relation to the St. Louis commons, says, the bounds of the commons began where the ox-mill now is, and thence west, up the hill; thence southwardly, in the rear of where Joseph Papen now lives; after it crossed Mill Creek, it went to the Prairie des Noyer; thence southwardly, about an arpent or two below the place called the Pain Sucre, which place is a little in the rear of where the shottower now is; and eastwardly by the Mississippi, passing by the spring of Beneto Vasquez. And this deponent says, that for upwards of sixty years the land contained within these limits was the St. Louis commons, and he believes was granted by St. Ange; and he does not live in St. Louis, nor has any lot there.

BAPTISTE his + mark. RIVIERE.

Sworn to before me, November 23d, 1825.

THEODORE HUNT, Recorder of Land Titles.

M. P. Leduc, being duly sworn, says he has truly translated and read the above the Baptiste Riviere.

M. P. LEDUC.

THEODORE HUNT, Recorder of Land Titles.

Pierre Chouteau, senior, being duly sworn, as relates to the St. Louis commons, says, that he came to this town about six months after the foundation of the same, and from that time he, of his knowledge, knows that the commons was recognized and allowed by the different lieutenant-governors, as well French as Spanish; and he further says, that as the town enlarged, there were meetings held of the inhabitants at the lieutenant-governor's, for the purpose of enlarging the commons. This was done more than once, and, as it was determined on at said meetings, the fence was removed, so as to enlarge the same for the use of the inhabitants of said town of St. Louis; and he further says, all land lying between the common field fence (excepting the ancient concession) and the river was considered as commons for the use of the inhabitants of St. Louis. He, this deponent, further says, that about twelve years ago he understood that Madame Laquaifee had a lot at the upper part of the town, adjoining the half moon battery, but before that time he never heard of such a claim, and he, of his knowledge, knows it never was possessed or occupied by any person before or at the time the change of government took place from France to the United States.

PRE. CHOUTEAU.

Sworn to before me, November 24th 1825.

THEODORE HUNT, Recorder of Land Titles.

See Hunt's minutes, book No. 3, pages 84 and 85.

Joseph Papen, being produced by Baptiste Douchonquette, was duly sworn, and says that he was born in the town of St. Louis, and is forty-five years of age, and has always lived in said town of St. Louis; that to the knowledge of this deponent there was no inclosure or common field lots below the town of St. Louis This deponent further says, that he is the grandson of Veuve Chouteau, the mother of Auguste Chouteau, and recollects perfectly well, that, when a small boy, the hands of the then commandant drove the hands of his grandmother from off the land which his grandmother claimed, below the town of St. Louis, called the Little Prairie; and further this deponent says, he never heard of the claims of Ortes, and Cambras, and Gervais, that is said was situated in this same prairie.

JOSEPH PAPIN.

Sworn to belore me, August 29th, 1825.

THEODORE HUNT, Recorder of Land Titles.

Francis Caillon, being duly sworn, says he has resided in the town of St. Louis for fifty-eight years, and to his knowledge there never was an inclosure in the Little Prairie south of the town of St. Louis. About thirty-five years ago, to the knowledge of this deponent, Madame Chouteau sent a man, Dubois, to cultivate the land she claimed in the said Little Prairie, and to the knowledge of this deponent, the then citizens of St. Louis complained to Perez, the then commandant [-] forbid that any inclosures or cultivation should be made there, and they immediately desisted; and this deponent says, he never has heard of any attempt to cultivate or inclose and of the said Little Prairie, south of the town of St. Louis. This deponent further says, that he was well acquainted with Ortes, and Cambras, and Gervais, and, to his knowledge, they, nor neither of them, ever did inclose, or cultivate, or claim any land in this said Little Prairie, south of the town of St. Louis.

FRANCOIS his + mark. CAILLON.

Sworn to before me, August 29th, 1825.

THEODORE HUNT, Recorder of Land Titles.

Baptiste Domin e, being duly sworn, says he has resided in the town of St. Louis for forty-five years, being occasionally absent for three or four months at a time, and, to his knowledge, during these forty-five years, there never was any land inclosed or cultivated in the Little Prairie, south of the town of St. Louis.

BAPTISTE his + mark. DOMINE.

Sworn to before me, August 29th, 1825.

THEODORE HUNT, Recorder of Land Titles.

Regis Vasseur, being duly sworn, says he has resided in the town of St. Louis for forty-eight years, and during the whole of this time the Little Prairie, south of the town of St. (Louis) belonged to the inhabitants of said

town as a commons, and during this time never was cultivated or inclosed.
REGIS his + mark. VASSEUR.
Sworn to before me, August 29th, 1825.
THEODORE HUNT, Recorder of Land Titles.
Horatio Cozens, being duly sworn, --- that he has translated and explained truly the above depositions to Joseph Papen, Francois Caillon, Baptiste Domine, and Regis Vasseur, respectively, before they swore to the same.
HORATIO COZENS.
Sworn to before me, August 29th, 1825.
THEODORE HUNT, Recorder of Land Titles.
See Hunt's minutes, book No. 2, pages 171-173.
RECORDER'S OFFICE,
St. Louis, Missouri, 5th Sept., 1839.
I certify the foregoing, in part, to be truly copied from the original documents on file, and the balance to be truly transcribed from the books all on file and of record in this office, being a full and complete transcript of all that appears of record in this office in relation to the claim of the inhabitants of the town of St. Louis to a common.
F. R. CONWAY, United States Recorder of Land Titles in the State of Missouri.
To the admission of all this evidence the plaintiff objected, which objection the court overruled; to which decision of the court overruling the objection of plaintiff, and admitting said documents in evidence, plaintiff excepted, and prayed that said exception be allowed, signed, and sealed by the court here and made part of the record in this cause.
Signed, EZRA HUNT. [SEAL.]
6. Act of Congress passed January 27th, 1831. (4 Lit. and Brown's ed. 435.)
This act declared,-'That the United States do hereby relinquish to the inhabitants of the several towns or villages of Portage des Sioux, St. Charles, St. Louis, andc., andc., all the right, title, and interest of the United States in and to the town or village lots, out lots, common field lots, and commons, in, adjoining, and belonging to the said towns or villages, confirmed to them respectively by the first section of the act of Congress, entitled, andc., passed on the 13th day of June, 1812.'
In the course of the trial a transcript of a record and deed were offered in evidence on the part of the defendant, and objected to by the plaintiff. The court sustained the objection, to which opinion the defendant excepted; but the Supreme Court having no jurisdiction of the matter, it is unnecessary to notice it further.
7. Evidence of Pascal Cerre.
'Pascal Cerre, being sworn, on his oath stated:-I have resided in St. Louis I may say since 1787. I was then fourteen years of age. I was a boy before then,-and was in St. Louis before then,-but cannot say that I remember any

thing except since 1787. I was pretty familiar with the tract of land called St. Louis commons, since 1787, and also acquainted with Mr. Mackay's claim, from the time he built his brick house. The land lying south of the Chouteau mill tract was owned by the inhabitants of St. Louis, or most of them, as a common. I knew the situation of the Barriere des Noyers field,- but not the situation of the common fence in relation thereto. I cannot tell whether common fence was west of Mackay's claim. The common fence began at the windmill, which is at the upper end of the town of St. Louis, at Menard house, betwixt the windmill and ox-mill, and run up in a western direction, passing by a little mound south of Ashley's premises to the front line of the forty arpents tract; then south along that line, near Madame Leioux, now Colonel Johnson's premises; then took a west direction towards the mill-pond, and went by a place used to be called Motard's plantation, now ----- from then it went west to the front line of the forty arpents in Prairie des Noyers, in a southeast direction from Fontaine's house, and running south passed by the spring in A. Gamble's, now McDonald's, plantation ten or twenty feet east of said spring; then in a southern direction to the northeast corner of the Carondelet common field; and thence I heard the Carondelet fence joined in, and went to the River des Peres. From the northeast corner of the Carondelet field, the fence went eastwardly to ----- now the shot-factory. The house where Mackay lived and died is now the convent. The land that lies west, to wit, the land described in the United States survey as Mackay's claim, between the line there designated and dotted as front boundary of St. Louis commons and Motard, on the west of said claim, was used as common, as well as the balance of the common. Motard's place is in the Cul-de-Sac, north of the fence. Where the spring of Motard is and his house was north of the fence; and Motard had no improvement south of the fence. The common fence never went to Stokes's place before it turned south, but went more to the left. There was no improvement south of Motard's fence; but all was brush and commons. The western part of the United States survey was always used as commons for grazing, to separate the cattle from the common fields, which were open. The inhabitants of the village got their wood on said land used as commons, when there was timber on it. My father did so. The land included in Mackay's survey, which was shown to witness, was used as commons until 1796 until the reign of Zenon Trudeau, when they ceased fencing the same as commons. It was continued to be used as wood and pasturage from that till 1804, and since. I believe that after 1796 all the country around St. Louis was used as common and indiscriminately, whether within or without the limits of where the commons fence stood. I went within the commons to get horses and hunt while the fence stood. There were plantations on the bank of the Mississippi,-Brazeau, Tayon, and others. Brazeau, Tayon, and others had separate fences, including all their cultivated ground, but did not go west further than the Carondelet road, which run then more easterly than now. My father had property within the commons, seventy-two arpents; he had a fence on it at all times until now. Vasquez had formerly a cabin in the commons, east of A. Gamble's, in the commons where Carr Lane now owns. A negro man lived in the cabin, and had a small inclosure, and was called Benete's spring,-la fontaine a Ben ete. He lived there in 1788 and 1789. I don't know whether he had a concession. Brazeau, Joseph, had property within the commons, and his fence there, his family and stock. Settlement, I knew of none but the settlement the negro lived in, within the commons, west of the Carondelet road. The other plantations went no further west than the Carondelet road. The Soulard property, which came from my father, went back to the Carondelet road, and no farther. I do not know that horses were continued to be pastured at liberty, except on the commons. I only heard of Mackay's claim till about twenty-four or twenty-five years ago, when he went and built his house. I have heard of Marie Nicol claim, which went by the name of Lefeore de Marie Ni Colle. It is in the commons on the northeast end of the commons, west of William Russell's, or rather northwest. The common fence was in good order in 1787. In 1782 I was in St. Louis, but can [not] say whether the fence was there.'

8. Two deeds from the city of St. Louis to Dent and Dillon respectively. The deed to Dillon was dated on the 7th of April, 1836.

To the admitting of which in evidence plaintiffs objected; which objection the court overruled; to which judgment of the court overruling the objection of plaintiffs, and admitting said documents in evidence, plaintiffs excepted. Here the defendant closed this cause.

Thereupon defendant moved the court to give the jury the following instruction:

'That the claim of the inhabitants of the town of St. Louis to commons, as exhibited upon the copy of the claim given in evidence, was confirmed by the act of Congress of the 13th June, 1812, to the inhabitants of said town according to the claim, and that the title to the land so confirmed is a valid title against the title of the plaintiffs under the confirmation, by the act of Congress of the 4th July, 1836.'

Given,-to the giving of which instruction plaintiffs objected; which objection the court overruled; to which judgment of the court overruling plaintiff's objection, and giving the said instructions, plaintiffs excepted; and thereupon plaintiffs moved the court to give the jury the following instructions:

'That Mackay's survey of common, preserving Mackay's claim on the northeast part thereof, is conclusive that the claim of commons did not extend over Mackay's claim, as between those claiming the common and Mackay or his heirs. That Mackay's survey of commons, including his claim, is good evidence to go to the jury that the claim of commons did not extend over and cover Mackay's claim. That the deed from the city to Dent conveyed no title under which defendant may justify in this action. That the deed from the city to Dillon conveyed no title under which defendant may justify in this action.'Refused,-all and each of which instructions the court refused to give; to which judgment of the court overruling plaintiff's motion, and refusing to give the said instructions, or any of them, plaintiffs excepted. These were all the instructions asked for, or given, or refused. And plaintiffs pray that their said several exceptions herein contained and set forth may be allowed, signed, and sealed by the court here, and made part of the record in this cause.

EZRA HUNT. [SEAL.]

The other bill of exceptions is in the words and figures following, to wit:

'ISABELLA MACKAY ET AL. v. PATRICK M. DILLON.

'Ejectment.

'ST. CHARLES CIRCUIT COURT:

'Be it remembered that plaintiffs moved the court for reasons filed, to wit:

'ISABELLA MACKAY ET AL. v. PATRICK M. DILLON.

'Ejectment.

'Plaintiffs move the court to set aside the verdict rendered in this cause, and grant them a new trial, because,

'1st. The court misinstructed the jury.

'2d. Because the court refused to give the instructions prayed for by plaintiffs.

'3d. Because the jury found against law and evidence.

'4th. Because the jury found against the weight of evidence.

'5th. Because the court admitted evidence that ought to have been excluded.

'6th. The allusions and instructions of the court operated as a surprise upon the plaintiffs.

'Isabella Mackay et al., plaintiffs, by their attorney, Bryan Mullanphy, moved the court to set aside the verdict in this cause, and grant them a new trial, which motion the court overruled; to which judgment of the court overruling said motion, and refusing to set aside said verdict, and grant plaintiffs a new trial, plaintiffs excepted; all evidence and matters in the cause being preserved in a previous bill of exceptions in this cause, plaintiffs pray that this exception now here taken be allowed, signed, and sealed by the court here, and made part of the record in this cause.

'EZRA HUNT. [SEAL.]'

Under these instructions of the court, the jury found a verdict for the defendant; and upon the bills of exceptions the case was carried up to the Supreme Court of Missouri, which, on the 24th of May, 1841, affirmed the judgment of the court below.

To review this opinion and judgment, a writ of error brought the case to this court.

The cause was argued by Mr. Lawless, for the plaintiff in error, and Mr. Gamble and Mr. Bates, for the defendant in error. The great but necessary length of the statement by the reporter renders it impossible to report these arguments, which were printed, and occupied forty pages.

Mr. Justice CATRON delivered the opinion of the court.

The record before us is brought here by a writ of error to the Supreme Court of Missouri, under the twenty-fifth section of the judiciary act. The action was an ejectment for land, to which each party claimed title by virtue of an act of Congress confirming interfering Spanish claims.

The evidence on part of the plaintiffs having been introduced in the State court of original jurisdiction, the defendant offered to read copies of certain documents and depositions taken in 1806 and 1825, certified by the United States recorder of land titles in the State of Missouri, as truly copied from the originals on file and of record in his office. These were objected to, on the part of the plaintiffs, as incompetent to go the jury; the objection was overruled, the evidence admitted, and an exception taken. And the first question is, was the evidence thus offered competent? It is set out in the report of the case, and need not be further described. As the objection draws in question the nature and character of the evidence, it is deemed proper to state here what they are; less for the purpose of disposing of the ruling of the court on this point, than as preparatory to the decision of others that follow, each involving the effect and character of the evidence more or less.

By the third article of the treaty of 1803, by which Louisiana was acquired, the inhabitants were to be maintained and protected in the free enjoyment of their property in the ceded territory. To carry the treaty into execution, as regarded titles and claims to land, Congress, by the act of March 2d, 1805, provided that a board of commissioners should be appointed by the President, and also a recorder of land titles; which was accordingly done. The board for Louisiana (now Missouri and Arkansas) sat at St. Louis, as at that place the recorder's office was established, and is yet kept.

By the fourth section of the act, all those asserting claims to land founded on concessions or other assumptions of right to obtain titles from the United States, and which claims originated with the French or Spanish governments prior to the 20th of December, 1803, were required, on or before the 1st day of March, 1806, to deliver to the recorder written notices of claim, stating the nature and extent thereof, together with a plat of the tract claimed, and written evidences tending to establish the right. The notice, plat, and evidences were to be recorded in books to be kept by the recorder for that purpose. This recorded notice and evidence formed the foundation in each case for the action of the board; although other evidence might be required by it, or be adduced by the claimant. The board was to decide in a summary way, according to justice and equity, on all claims thus filed.

It was directed to appoint a clerk, whose duty it should be to enter in book full and correct minutes of the proceedings and decisions of the board; together with the evidence on which each decision was made; the book, on the dissolution of the board, was to be deposited with the recorder of land titles; but the clerk was first to make two copies, one of which he was to forward to the Secretary of the Treasury, and the other was to be deposited with the surveyor-general in said district. According to this law, the inhabitants of St. Louis filed their notice of claim, plat, and evidences, in 1806, asking to have the town common confirmed to them.

By the first section of the act of 1812 (June 13th), Congress confirmed the claim to commons adjoining and belonging to St. Louis; with similar claims made by other towns. But no extent or boundaries were given to show what land was granted; nor is there any thing in the act of 1812, from which a court of justice can legally declare that the land set forth by the survey, and proved as commons by witnesses, in 1806, is the precise land Congress granted; in other words, the act did not adopt the evidence laid before the board for any purpose; and the boundaries of claims thus confirmed were designedly (as we suppose) left open to the settlement of the respective claimants, by litigation in the courts of justice, or otherwise.

The confirmation extended to town lots, out lots, common field lots, and commons in, adjoining, or belonging to the several towns or villages. And the act of 1812 made it the duty of the principal deputy-surveyor of the territory, as soon thereafter as might be, to survey, or cause it to be done, and marked, the out-boundary lines of the several towns, so as to include the out lots, common field lots, and commons; of this out-boundary survey, he was to make plats, and transmit them to the surveyor-general, who was to forward copies to the commissioner of the general land-office and to the United States recorder of land titles in Missouri. The object of this proceeding, on part of the government, was to sever the confirmed claims in a mass from the remaining lands of the United States, and others outside of the boundary, and nothing more.

The act of May 26th, 1824, supplemental to that of 1812, authorized further proofs to be taken before the recorder in regard to town lots, out lots, and common field lots, confirmed by the act of 1812, as respected inhabitation, cultivation, or possession, and the boundaries and extent of each claim; but the provision does not extend in terms to the commons. In virtue of this act, however, the evidence found in the record, and taken before the recorder in 1825, was filed in the recorder's office further to establish the extent of the town commons.

The objection taken in the State Circuit Court was to the whole evidence certified from the recorder's office, without discrimination, and the question turns on its competency for any purpose.

The powers of the Supreme Court are limited in cases coming up from the State courts, under the twenty-fifth section of the judiciary act, to questions of law, where the final judgment or decree draws in question the validity of a treaty or statute of the United States, andc., or where their construction is drawn in question, or an authority exercised under them; and as the admission of evidence to establish the mere fact of boundary in regard to the extent of grant cannot raise a question involving either the validity or construction of an act of Congress, andc., this court has no jurisdiction to consider and revise the decision of a State court, however erroneous it may be in admitting the evidence to establish the fact. But when evidence is admitted as competent for this purpose, and it is sought to give it effect for other purposes which do involve questions giving this court jurisdiction, then the decisions of State courts on the effect of such evidence may be fully considered here, and their judgments reversed or affirmed, in a similar manner as if a like question had arisen in a supreme court of error of a State, when reversing the proceedings of inferior courts of original jurisdiction,-and on this principle we are compelled to act in the present suit, when dealing with the instruction given on behalf of the defendant.

2. The following instructions were next asked on part of the plaintiffs, and refused:-'That Mackay's survey of common, preserving Mackay's claim on the northeast part thereof, is conclusive that the claim of commons did not extend over Mackay's claim, as between those claiming the common and Mackay or his heirs. That Mackay's survey of commons, including his claim, is good evidence to go to the jury, that the claim of commons did not extend over and cover Mackay's claim.'

The survey referred to was the one made in 1806, at the instance of the inhabitants of St. Louis, for the purpose of presenting their claim to commons in due form to the board. It was in its nature a private survey, not binding on the United States; and to avoid any implication to the contrary, the act of February 28th, 1806, was passed, which extended the powers of the surveyor-general of Louisiana over the land in controversy, and made it his duty to appoint principal deputies; over these, the commissioners at St. Louis had power given to them, by which surveys could be ordered of private claims. When the board desired surveys to be made, they ordered them to be executed at the expense of the party interested. And the law declares, that every such survey, as well as every other survey, by whatever authority heretofore executed (those of legal and complete titles only excepted), shall be held and considered as private surveys only; and all tracts of land, the titles to which may be ultimately confirmed by Congress, shall, prior to the issuing of patents, be resurveyed, if judged necessary, under the authority of the surveyor-general. It follows, that Mackay's survey of 1806 had no influence on the title of either party, and that the instructions asked were properly refused.

3. The following instruction was asked for, and given, on part of the defendants:-'That the claim of the inhabitants of the town of St. Louis to commons, as exhibited upon the copy of the claim given in evidence, was confirmed, by the act of Congress of the 13th of June, 1812, to the inhabitants of said town, according to the claim, and that the title to the land so confirmed is a valid title against the title of the plaintiffs under the confirmation, by the act of Congress of the 4th of July, 1836.'

It assumes, as matter of law, that the act of 1812 adopted Mackay's survey, and the evidence given in its support; that they are part of the grant, as to its extent and legal effect; and conclusive as against the plaintiff' confirmation. On the trial, both parties admitted that the land in dispute lies within the survey of 1806, and therefore the instruction took the case from the jury, and cut off all proof to the contrary of this being the true boundary; whereas the survey was a mere private act, as already stated, and concluded nothing for either side; and in holding the contrary the State court erred, and for which the judgment must be reversed.

By what description of surveys the United States are bound, and those claiming title under them governed, we have already, during the present term, been called on to decide, in the case of Jourdan v. Barrett (ante, p. 169), and need not repeat. Nor is it necessary to inquire here what the effect of a legal survey of the St. Louis common is, as the question has been directly presented in the cause of Les Bois v. Bramell, heard and decided concurrently with this, and on the same arguments, and to the opinion in which, in this respect, we refer.

www.ingramcontent.com/pod-product-compliance
Lightning Source LLC
Chambersburg PA
CBHW070756180526
45168CB00004B/1641